WORLD: BMX and Mountain Biking

Paul Mason

A&C Black • London

Produced for A & C Black by
Monkey Puzzle Media Ltd
48 York Avenue
Hove BN3 1PJ, UK

Published by A & C Black Publishers
Limited, 36 Soho Square,
London W1D 3QY

First published 2010

ISBN 978-1-4081-2772-8

A CIP catalogue record for this book is
available from the British Library.

Editor: Dan Rogers
Design: Mayer Media Ltd
Picture research: Lynda Lines

This book is produced using paper that
is made from wood grown in managed,
sustainable forests. It is natural,
renewable and recyclable. The logging
and manufacturing processes conform
to the environmental regulations of the
country of origin.

Printed and bound in China by C&C
Offset Printing Co.

Picture acknowledgements
Alamy pp. 14 (Eric Lawton), 15 (Ultimate
Group LLC), 16 (Seb Rogers); Corbis pp.
12 (Kennan Harvey/Aurora Open), 29
(Vocal Image Communications/Brand X);
Getty Images pp. 1 (Scott Markewitz), 5,
6 (Philip Kaake), 28 (Scott Markewitz);
iStockphoto p. 9; Chris Kovarik p. 4;
Matthew Lee p. 24; Paul Mason pp. 7,
11, 13, 17, 21; Matt McFee p. 25 top;
MPM Images p. 20; PA Photos p. 23 (Tim
Johnson/Landov); Rex Features p. 27
(Sipa Press); Keith Romanowski p. 26;
Alex Schelbert pp. 18, 19; Shutterstock
pp. 24 top (Dario Sabljak), 25 top
right (Dario Sabljak); Martin Strasser
p. 10; Aaron Teasdale p. 25 bottom;
Teignbridge District Council, South
Devon p. 8; Topfoto p. 22 (Polfoto).
Compass rose artwork on front cover
and inside pages by iStockphoto. Map
artwork by MPM Images.

The front cover shows a mountain biker
getting airborne on a fast downhill run
(iStockphoto).

SAFETY ADVICE

Don't attempt any of the
activities or techniques
in this book without the
guidance of a qualified
instructor.

CONTENTS

It's a Two-Wheeled World   4

Marin County   6

Decoy   8

Semmering   10

Durango   12

Camp Woodward   14

Afan Valley   16

The BMX Worlds   18

Mount Beauty   20

Copenhagen   22

Tour Divide MTB Race   24

New York City   26

Les Deux Alpes   28

Glossary   30

Finding Out More   31

Index   32

It's a Two-Wheeled World

Your bike is balanced at the top of a steep slope, the front wheel just short of starting to roll downwards. All it takes is a little push with your foot, and there's no going back. Your stomach does a loop-the-loop, as you lean forwards and drop downwards at breath-stealing speed. This is the thrill-a-minute world of BMX and mountain biking.

A hard-cornering rider throws his bike into a banked turn.

PASSPORT TO BMX AND MOUNTAIN BIKING

This book is your passport to the worlds of BMX and mountain biking. You can find out the secret words that riders use, their special techniques (from beginner to expert level), and the equipment they use. Most of all, this book is a guide to where to ride: the places you'd go if you could travel anywhere in the two-wheeled world.

THE SECRET LANGUAGE OF BIKING

berm banked-up bend on a BMX or mountain-bike track
ollie jump

Dropping into a BIG half pipe on a BMX — full-face helmets and pads are required on a ramp like this!

RIDING WORLD

Whatever kind of riding you want to do, there's a place that's perfect for practising your skills. Want to improve your downhill **berm**-riding ability? Desperate to learn how to **ollie** or funky chicken on your BMX? This book shows you the best places to practise all kinds of BMX and mountain biking techniques.

 ## Technical: Riding styles and machines

This book deals with four main types of riding: BMX, cross-country (XC), freeride and downhill mountain biking. Each uses slightly different bikes.

BMX:	Cross-country:	Freeride:	Downhill:
BMX bikes have small frames, high handlebars, one gear, no suspension and 20-inch wheels.	XC bikes are relatively light, and have front suspension (a few also have rear suspension). Like nearly all mountain bikes (MTBs) they have 26-inch wheels.	Freeride bikes are designed for general riding, plus jumps and drop-offs. They are similar to XC bikes, but tougher and heavier.	Downhill bikes are heavy and very, very strong. They are designed to cope with big impact at high speed. Most have front and rear suspension.

Marin County

Where better to enjoy your first experiences of mountain biking than the place where it was invented? Marin County is sometimes known as the birthplace of mountain biking. In the 1970s, people began racing old **cruiser** bikes down Marin's Mount Tamalpais. Then they started adapting the bikes so that they were better at going off-road. Before long, a whole new kind of bike – the mountain bike – had been invented.

MARIN COUNTY
Location: California, USA
Type of riding: XC
Difficulty level: 1.5 of 5
Best season: year-round, but best May to September.

The coastal trails and wooded valleys of Marin County make riding here a great experience, especially for cross-country mountain biking.

WHY MARIN?

The cross-country trails through Marin's redwood forests are a great way to start enjoying the sport. In all there are 400 kilometres (250 miles) of marked trails, so there's never any chance of getting bored. And being in California, there's a good chance the sun will be shining, too.

THE SECRET LANGUAGE OF BIKING

cruiser old-style bike with upright riding position

singletrack path wide enough for only one bike

If you like Marin...

... you could also try:

- Laggan Wolftrax, Scotland
- Blue Mountains, Australia

Both offer great riding in woodland.

WHERE TO RIDE

Beginners: The Shoreline Trail winds its way through the woodland bordering San Pablo Bay. Mainly on **singletrack** paths, there are thrills as well as great views.

Improvers and experts: The 28-kilometre (17-mile) Eldridge Grade to East Peak Loop winds its way up Mount Tamalpais before a fast descent. Or try the area's most remote route, the Pine Mountain Loop, which has some tight, technical sections.

Tip from a Local

This is a great place to spend a whole day exploring: take plenty of water and a packed lunch.

SKILL

Sizing a bike

Whether you're hiring or buying a mountain bike, it's important for comfort and safety that it's the right size:

1. Stand astride the bike. You should have a 10–20 centimetre (4–8 inch) gap between the top tube and your crotch.

2. Sitting on the saddle (leaning against a wall is safest), put one pedal in its lowest possible position. If the saddle is at the right height, your foot should be able to just rest on the pedal without stretching your leg.

3. The handlebars should be at about the same height as the saddle, so that you ride along with your arms slightly bent. This may be hard to get right on a rented bike, but it is less important than the other two measurements.

Decoy

The rolling countryside and wooded valleys of the English county of Devon probably aren't where you'd expect to find one of England's best BMX venues. Nonetheless, travel to the small town of Newton Abbot, and that's exactly what you'll find.

Taking part in a competition at Decoy; skaters and BMXers mix happily side by side here.

Tip from a Local
If you're going into the concrete park, watch out for the Splat Bowl – it didn't get the name by accident!

WHY DECOY?
Decoy is unusual in that you can go there and try practically any kind of BMX riding. If you want to improve your ramp riding or street tricks, there's an excellent BMX and skatepark. Decoy also has a BMX race track: you can take the **pegs** off your bike, put on a full-face helmet and some armour, and have a go.

DECOY
Location: Devon, England
Type of riding: BMX, mixed
Difficulty level: 1.5 of 5
Best season: all year, but warmest/driest June to September

WHERE TO RIDE

BMX: The track was first opened in 1998, and whatever your ability it is rideable. A recent redesign has brought it up to date.

Park: Opened in 2008, the concrete bowls of the park area will have ramp riders drooling.

Dirt jump: Decoy also has excellent **dirt jumps** – as you would expect at a place designed with the help of former BMX world dirt-jump champion Kye Forte.

THE SECRET LANGUAGE OF BIKING

peg tube of metal attached to the wheel axle of a BMX bike.

dirt jump large jump that keeps the rider airborne for a long time

If you like Decoy...

... you could also try:

• Camp Woodward and Woodward West, USA
Both have track, park and street BMX facilities in one place.

SKILL
Ollies

Ollies – jumps, either from flat ground or a ramp – are a basic BMX skill. There are many complicated versions of an ollie, but here's how to do a basic one:

The first rule of learning new tricks: START SMALL, like this rider. Then you can go bigger once you've got the basics right.

1. With the bike rolling forward, stand up on the pedals. Both pedals should be at the same height.

2. Pull up on the bars, aiming to lift the front wheel off the ground.

3. Lean forwards and let the back wheel come up into the air. Some riders roll their wrists forwards while holding the bars tight, to help the back wheel lift up.

4. Lean back and allow the bike to land, either on the back wheel or both wheels together.

Ollies can take a while to learn smoothly, but once you've managed it, you'll be riding around wearing a big grin for days.

Semmering

Semmering is typical of lots of small villages in the European Alps – mountain biking has recently become a popular summer activity. What's different about Semmering is that the routes have all been planned so that beginners can have a go – even the specially designed freeride and downhill courses.

SEMMERING
Location: Austria
Type of riding: all types
Difficulty level: 1.5 of 5
Best season: June to September

A rider hurtles along the downhill course at Semmering, Austria.

WHY SEMMERING?

This is a great place for a first visit to a bikepark and for practising **freeride** skills. Beginners will be able to handle most of the raised wooden sections, berms and drops. Once they have got used to these, it's time to try the freeride course that runs from the top to the bottom of the mountain.

Tip from a Local

Avoid riding here if it's very wet – the trails get very muddy and hard to ride.

Technical: Kit checklist

It is possible to ride wearing ordinary clothes, but a few pieces of specialist kit make mountain biking more comfortable and safer. The rider below is wearing several bits of really useful gear.

Helmet (or "skid lid") – the single most important bit of equipment.

Glasses – protect your eyes from dirt, flies, water, etc. Also stop your eyes filling with tears when going fast, making it easier to see.

Backpack – for carrying spares, tools, food, extra clothes, etc. These often have a compartment for storing water, which can be sucked out using a tube.

Gloves – full-finger or fingerless, these usually have padding where your hands rest against the handlebars.

Shorts – with padded section where your body rubs against the saddle.

Shoes – some riders use shoes with a special plate on the sole that attaches to the pedals.

Biking jersey – these tend to be fairly close fitting (but not tight). In summer a short-sleeved one is fine; in winter, long sleeves, thermals underneath, and a jacket may also be needed!

THE SECRET LANGUAGE OF BIKING

freeride riding over jumps, ramps and other artificial obstacles

If you like Semmering...

… you could also try:
• Vancouver Island, Canada
It has great freeriding.

WHERE TO RIDE

Beginners: Will want to start off on the family route, which is a simple introduction to Semmering, or perhaps to do one of the XC tours of the area.

Improvers and experts: The most challenging riding in Semmering is on the downhill racecourse. This would be challenging on anything but a downhill bike, and is certainly not ideal for inexperienced riders.

Durango

You could spend a year in Durango and probably still not have time to ride all the trails. Even though it's rated one of the top ten ski resorts in the USA, Durango is actually busier in the summer – mainly because it's full of mountain bikers. This is one of North America's hottest mountain-bike destinations.

DURANGO
Location: Colorado, USA
Type of riding: mainly XC
Difficulty level: 2.5 of 5
Best season: May to October

WHY DURANGO?

There is probably more cross-country riding than anything else in Durango. Even so, there is something for every kind of rider. The San Juan Mountains offer plenty of opportunity to stretch your legs in long climbs, followed by much quicker downhills.

Tip from a Local

If you fancy a change for the day, take a trip to Telluride – it's just up the road, and the riding is almost as good.

Cadence is the speed at which you turn the pedals when you're riding. Getting your cadence right is a key bike-riding skill:

If you like Durango...

... you could also try:
- Sierra Nevada, Spain

It has a similar landscape and trails.

• Most riders aim for a cadence of between 80 and 120 pedal strokes per minute. (Every time either the left or right-hand pedal reaches the bottom of its spin, that counts as one stroke.)

WHERE TO RIDE

Beginners: Practise your uphill riding skills on the Dry Fork Loop. This singletrack trail through the San Juan National Forest contains a 2.5-kilometre (1.5-mile) uphill section.

• While riding uphill, especially on a mountain bike, keep your cadence in the higher range.

Improvers and experts: The 30-kilometre (18.5-mile) Hermosa Creek Trail is one of the USA's best cross-country routes. The mostly downhill path follows the route of Hermosa Creek – and steep drops down towards the water mean this is not a good place to **bail**.

• For riding downhill, a lower cadence is OK, because gravity will help you speed up if you need to.

THE SECRET LANGUAGE OF BIKING

bail jump off in order to avoid crashing

It might be steep going up – but that means this Durango route will probably be steep going down, too!

Camp Woodward

For years, many kids in the USA have spent a week or more of the school holidays at summer camp. Camp Woodward is a summer camp with a difference – it's dedicated to extreme sports. Every year, young BMXers head for Woodward to pick up new skills.

The best training for BMX racing is racing – just what these students at the Woodward summer camp are doing.

CAMP WOODWARD
Location: Pennsylvania, USA
Type of riding: BMX, all types
Difficulty level: 1.5 of 5
Camp open: June to August

If you like Camp Woodward...

... you could also try:
- Woodward West, California, USA
It offers more of the same.

LEARN FROM THE PROS

One of the big attractions of the Woodward summer camps is that among the instructors there are always a few **pro** riders. Whatever your age or ability – from 7-year-old beginner to 18-year-old expert – there will be an instructor who can help you develop your BMX skills. The camp runs training sessions both for racing and for freestyle.

THE SECRET LANGUAGE OF BIKING

pro professional, someone who is paid to ride

Tip from a Local

If you can't afford to pay for a stay at Woodward, try applying for one of the scholarships that are available every year.

BMX HEAVEN

Woodward has a mind-blowing line-up of BMX facilities. The Big Dirt is a training ground for budding racers. Ramp riders will feel a sense of nervous excitement when they see the Mega Ramp, or Lot 8, for the first time. And for those who fancy a bit of street riding, there's a whole load of fun to be had in the Outdoor Street section. And these are just half of the camp's eight separate areas!

You not only get taught by pro riders at Woodward – you also get to watch them ride.

Afan Valley

South Wales was once a major UK coal-mining centre. The mountain valleys there are steep-sided, with thick pine forests and mossy rocks. This makes the area an atmospheric mountain-biking destination. The work of the local trail-builders makes it a truly thrilling one, too.

AFAN VALLEY
Location: Neath Port Talbot, Wales
Type of riding: MTB cross-country
Difficulty level: 3.5 of 5
Best season: June to Sept is driest

WHY AFAN?

Most riders new to Afan follow the specially designed, waymarked bike routes. Not really suitable for beginners, these paths generally use **fire roads** to gain height, then zigzag their way back across and down the mountainside. Long singletrack sections, damp rocks and tree roots, and **gullies** carved by rainwater all make this a challenging place to ride.

If you like Afan Valley...

... you could also try:
• Glentress, Scotland
• Squamish, Canada
Both offer atmospheric forest riding.

Riders out for the long haul, tackling Afan's Skyline trail — 46 kilometres (28.6 miles) long, and with 2 kilometres (1.25 miles) of vertical ascent.

Uphill skills

Tip from a Local
Head for The Wall – one of the best singletrack descents in the UK.

The Afan trails generally get you uphill as easily as possible on fire roads, but you do still have to pedal! Some sections of each ride also require singletrack uphill skills.

• Pick your gear carefully. A higher cadence will allow you to slow down if the slope suddenly gets steeper or you have to pedal over an obstacle.

• Higher cadence also means you can stay seated as much as possible. This puts weight on the back wheel, giving extra grip and stopping the tyre from slipping.

• Bending your elbows and leaning forwards slightly helps the front tyre to stay on the ground. (Sitting up and pulling backwards on the handlebars while pedalling hard will make the front wheel lift off the ground.)

WHERE TO RIDE

Beginners: Afan is not really suitable for beginners.

Improvers: All four "hard"-graded routes at Afan are suitable for improvers. You need to be fit to tackle Skyline, in particular – at 46 kilometres (28.6 miles), it's a real challenge.

Experts: Will enjoy the red routes, but the biggest challenge is W2, which is graded "severe" and combines tough sections of two "hard" routes.

Other tips: Bring a waterproof! It does rain a lot here, but that needn't stop you riding.

THE SECRET LANGUAGE OF BIKING

fire road wide, smooth path meant to allow access for fire engines

gully ditch, which acts as a trap for your wheels

This rider is showing good technique for riding uphill: a high cadence, elbows bent and weight evenly spread between the wheels.

The BMX Worlds

Every year, the world's best BMX riders gather to take part in the Worlds, or world championships. These are not for BMX racers, who have their own event. This championship is for each of the five kinds of freestyle BMX: park, dirt jump, **vert ramp**, mini ramp and flatland.

THE BMX WORLDS
Location: changes each year
Type of riding: BMX, all kinds
Difficulty level: 5 of 5
Time of year: summer, usually July

THE SECRET LANGUAGE OF BIKING

vert ramp vert is short for vertical: a ramp with vertical sides
air jump or "aerial". "Big air" is a big jump.

Danny Josa pulls a massive air at the 2009 World BMX championships.

Anthony Napolitan – a graduate of Camp Woodward – flying high at the 2009 Worlds.

CONTEST EVENTS

Every kind of freestyle BMX contest happens at the Worlds. Males can take part in all the competitions, but female world champions are only crowned in flatland and park.

• **Flatland** A bit like watching a cross between break-dancing and ballet – on a BMX bike. The riders use amazing skills and balance to do things you never dreamed were possible on two wheels.

• **Park** A whole area of ramps allows the riders to put together a routine of aerials, grinds and spins to wow the judges.

• **Dirt jump** A set of big ramps made of (surprise!) dirt gives the riders a chance to get big **air**.

• **Vert ramp** Two large, vertical-walled ramps connected by a flat area. Vert is one of the most spectacular BMX events, with riders flying high into the air.

• **Mini ramp** Mini ramps are made of two short ramps connected to a flat area. Often two are used back-to-back, with a knife-edge between them, which makes for big gasps from the spectators.

Mount Beauty

High up in the Australian Alps, Mount Beauty is a ski resort in winter and one of Australia's top mountain biking venues in summer. The trails here are so good that this is where the 2007 Australian National Championships were held for Downhill and XC riding.

MOUNT BEAUTY
Location: Victoria, Australia
Type of riding: all kinds
Difficulty level: 3 of 5
Best season: all year-round, but best weather November to April

WHY MOUNT BEAUTY?

Mount Beauty is sometimes called Australia's mountain-biking capital. Most trails start right from town, meaning you can easily stock up on supplies before a long ride. In bad weather, the routes through the forests on the mountain's lower slopes offer shelter. On hot days, climbing up into the mountains takes you into the cooler air high up.

Mount Beauty has almost everything a mountain biker could want, from forested singletrack routes to wide-open countryside.

If you like Mount Beauty...

... you could also try:
• Innerleithen, Scotland
• Kranskja Gora, Slovenia
Both offer the chance to ride a national championship course.

THE SECRET LANGUAGE OF BIKING

inside the side closest to the direction of a turn

outside the side furthest from the direction of a turn

This rider has his eyes fixed on the "vanishing point", the spot in his vision where the two sides of the trail appear to meet. He is using it to judge his speed.

WHERE TO RIDE

Beginners: The annual race from Mitt-Mitta to Mount Beauty is designed for riders of all abilities. This would be a good way to get a taste of the XC race scene.

Improvers: The Dark Side, particularly Honeysuckle Gully, will challenge your bike-handling skills.

Experts: The national downhill trail zigs and zags its way down the slopes of Mount Beauty into the town.

On a route such as the national downhill track at Mount Beauty, cornering skills are crucial if you want to enjoy a smooth, safe ride. Here are a few tips that will help:

• If riding downhill, lowering the saddle height will put more weight on to the back tyre, giving extra grip.

• Judge your speed by looking at the point where the two sides of the trail meet in your vision. If this point seems to be moving towards you, slow down. If it gets further away, speed up!

• Bend your **inside** elbow more than the **outside** one. This puts your weight over the tyres and gives extra grip.

• As the bike leans into the turn, extend your outside leg so that the pedal is as low as possible. This gives better grip and stops the inside pedal snagging on obstacles such as rocks.

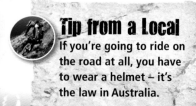

Tip from a Local
If you're going to ride on the road at all, you have to wear a helmet – it's the law in Australia.

Copenhagen

For bikers of all kinds, Copenhagen is a must-visit destination. The city has been named an official Bike City by the UCI, cycle-sport's governing body. (So far, it is the ONLY Bike City!) Copenhagen regularly hosts a round of the BMX **Supercross** World Cup, and in 2011 will host both the world track and world BMX championships.

Flying high in Copenhagen, this rider has given his rivals the slip. Only a crash can stop him from winning.

COPENHAGEN
Location: Copenhagen, Denmark
Type of riding: BMX, track
Difficulty level: 2 of 5
Best season: May to September

WHY COPENHAGEN?

The BMX track in Copenhagen is one of the best in the world. The track was designed by top-level riders, and is right in the city centre. This is a great place to learn the basics of BMX racing. You can take part yourself, or watch some of the world's top racers hurtle down the start ramp at up to 60 kilometres per hour (37 miles per hour).

RIDING COPENHAGEN

The top riders whiz round the 300-metre (330-yard) track in about 30 seconds. If that sounds a bit quick to you, don't worry. One of the good things about Copenhagen is that some sections of the track are easier than others. It's possible to ride flat-out over those and then take it a bit easier over the tough bits.

22

If you like Copenhagen...

... you could also try:
- Madrid, Spain
- Chula Vista, California
- Fréjus, France

They all host BMX supercross races.

Riders begin a race down the massive start ramp of the 2008 Beijing Olympics BMX course.

Tip from a Local

In summer, you can ride late into the night – this far north, the sun barely sets.

THE SECRET LANGUAGE OF BIKING

supercross the highest level of BMX competition

SKILL
The hole shot

One of the most impressive (and perhaps intimidating) things about Copenhagen is the start ramp. At 8 metres (26 feet) high, it's quite a drop down towards the first bend – which everyone wants to get to first. The riders call this the hole shot.

1. The riders line up behind the start gate at the top of the ramp.

2. As the start gate drops, the riders lean forwards and pedal, accelerating as fast as possible down the ramp.

3. At high speed, they leap between the first peaks on the starting straight.

4. Whoever gets to the berm first has made the hole shot.

Making the hole shot gives you the advantage of a clear run through the turn and into the second straight. This makes it less likely you will get caught up in crashes.

Tour Divide MTB Race

TOUR DIVIDE
Location: North America
Type of riding: endurance mountain biking
Difficulty level: 5 of 5
Time of year: June to July

The Tour Divide race *might* not be the toughest mountain bike event in the world – but it's almost certainly the longest. The race begins in Banff, Canada, and finishes (usually about a month later) in Antelope Wells, USA. When they've finished, the competitors will have cycled 4418 kilometres (2745 miles), and climbed 61 000 metres (200 000 feet).

CHALLENGES OF THE ROUTE

Tour Divide riders face many challenges apart from the huge distance. The course is not marked, and winds along old, almost-forgotten trails, so you have to be an excellent navigator. The race passes through bear and mountain-lion country. Riders must find their own shelter, or **bivouac** by the side of the trail.

Riding along a mountain road in Montana, only about 2000 kilometres (1240 miles) to go!

Crossing the Red Desert, the massive distances
covered by Tour Divide racers really come into focus.

RULES OF THE ROAD

Most of the race rules are designed
to make sure that everyone races on
an equal basis. Anything that might
give one rider an unfair advantage is
banned. Key rules include:

• Riders must be self-supporting – no
help from outside is allowed.

• The only way you can move forwards
on the route is by pedalling or
walking. (If your bike breaks, you can
get a lift back, but not forwards.)

• You're on your own! There are no
race officials on the course, and there
is no pre-race briefing. You just turn
up and start riding with everyone else.

If you like the Tour Divide...

... you could also try:
• The TransRockies
race, Canada
• The TransWales race
• The TransScotland race
Each offers a long-haul
race experience.

Tour Divide racers need to be willing to get their feet (and legs,
arms, and body) wet – as this rider's about to find out.

New York City

NEW YORK CITY
Location: New York, USA
Type of riding: all kinds
Difficulty level: 4 of 5
Best season: all year – but it's COLD in winter!

New York City is of one of the world's most famous tourist destinations. It would make it into most people's top places to visit even if there was no riding here at all. Fortunately for keen BMXers, though, in New York the opportunities for freestyle are just as good as all the other sights.

WHY NEW YORK?

New York has a massive variety of places to ride. From super-famous spots like the Brooklyn Banks (see below) to places that only the local riders know about, there are opportunities for riding everywhere. Parks, ramps, **rails**, flatland – there's something for every kind of rider.

THE SECRET LANGUAGE OF BIKING

rail short for handrail, a metal bar along which you can slide the pegs

Street BMX is alive and kicking in almost every corner of New York City: almost anywhere you CAN ride, people DO.

Tip from a Local

Only ride where it's allowed – otherwise you risk being fined by a New York City police officer.

Technical: BMX etiquette

In New York, riding in the wrong place can get you a fine from a police officer, or worse. Just like everywhere, it pays to bear in mind a few simple guidelines:

• Always ride with good manners. Don't come racing up behind people who don't know you're there. Even if people are enjoying watching you do tricks, be careful not to get scary-close to them.

• Always ride within your own abilities: crashing will have serious effects not only on you, but also possibly on other people.

• Never ride where there are signs saying you shouldn't. "No skateboarding" signs are often a clue that BMXers won't be welcome either.

• Be careful not to damage property.

By following these guidelines, BMXers should be able to get along with non-riders, and keep the right to ride in their favourite spots.

Styling a combined peg and pedal grind.

WHERE TO RIDE

There are so many famous riding spots in New York that it's almost impossible to make a short list of them. But among the places not to be missed are:

Tompkins Square Park In the famous Lower East Side neighbourhood of Manhattan, this venue has a good flatland area, as well as excellent ramps.

Brooklyn Banks One of the world's most legendary BMX (and skateboard) spots, the Banks are in a park underneath the Brooklyn Bridge on the Manhattan Island side. They are threatened with closure because of construction work, so get there quick!

If you like New York City...

... you could also try:
• London, England
• Barcelona, Spain
They both offer a real big-city riding experience.

Les Deux Alpes

In recent years, Les Deux Alpes has become Europe's biggest and best mountain-biking resort. The town has embraced mountain biking as a summer activity and, as a result, it has excellent facilities. The purpose-built trails, good route marking, and lots of high-profile mountain-biking events make Les Deux Alpes a must-visit destination.

LES DEUX ALPES
Location: Isère, France
Type of riding: MTB, mixed
Difficulty level: 4 of 5
Best season: lifts open June to end August

One slip, and you're in the drink! But at least it'll be a soft landing — unlike a fall on most of Les Deux Alpes routes.

WHY LES DEUX ALPES?

There is good riding here for everyone. The routes range from tight, technical downhill **lines** for experts only, to XC trails that relative beginners can manage. And whatever kind of riding you want to do, it's available here. There are 15 cross-country routes, 18 downhill runs, and a bike park for freeriders.

Tip from a Local

Don't ride the jump trails on windy days – you might get blown sideways while you're airborne!

If you like Les Deux Alpes...

... you could also try:
• Whistler, Canada
The new Serre Palas trail is similar to Whistler's famous A-Line Trail.

SKILL
downhill tips

Full-on downhill trails really are for experts only. On many of them you need to be riding a specialist bike, and wearing body armour, to have a chance of getting to the bottom safely.

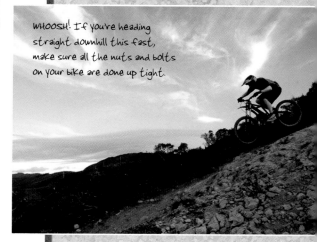

WHOOSH! If you're heading straight downhill this fast, make sure all the nuts and bolts on your bike are done up tight.

WHERE TO RIDE

Beginners: The easier cross-country routes (graded blue) are ideal for beginners: ask at the Tourist Office for a map of the trails.

Improvers: The Pied Moutet downhill route is a good introduction; the bike park has some easier lines built in for improvers to use.

Experts: Both the World Cup downhill trail and the Thuit trail are eyeballs-out scary.

Other tips: Bring sunglasses and sunscreen – the riding in Les Deux Alpes is nearly all out in the open.

• The lift attendant will load your bike on to the lift. Usually it is hooked on through the front wheel, so make sure the **quick releases** are done up tight!

• Once at the top, make sure your saddle is set lower than the handlebars. It may feel odd at first, but when you start off down a steep slope it will feel correct.

• Ride with two fingers on each brake lever at all times. That way, you will be able to slow down or stop immediately.

• On the trail, always look ahead, rather than down at the ground under your wheels. A full-suspension bike will deal with small obstacles on its own – it's the big ones that are visible from far away you need to watch out for.

THE SECRET LANGUAGE OF BIKING

line route or path

quick release lever on wheel axle to allow fast wheel removal

Glossary

Words from the Secret Language features

air jump or "aerial". "Big air" is a big jump.

bail jump off in order to avoid crashing

berm banked-up bend on a BMX or mountain-bike track

bivouac sleep outdoors in a temporary shelter

cruiser old-style bike with upright riding position

dirt jump large jump that keeps the rider airborne for a long time

fire road wide, smooth path meant to allow access for fire engines

freeride riding over jumps, ramps and other artificial obstacles

gully ditch, which acts as a trap for your wheels

inside the side closest to the direction of a turn

line route or path

ollie jump

outside the side furthest from the direction of a turn

peg tube of metal attached to the wheel axle of a BMX bike

pro professional, someone who is paid to ride

quick release lever on wheel axle to allow fast wheel removal

rail short for handrail, a metal bar along which you can slide the pegs

singletrack path wide enough for only one bike

supercross the highest level of BMX competition

vert ramp vert is short for vertical: a ramp with vertical sides

Other words riders use

blood donor an injured rider

clean ride a trail smoothly, without crashing

dab put your foot down to avoid crashing

face plant crash face first

grinder very steep hill

gutter bunny someone who cycles to work or school

session period of time spent riding at a place

snakebite double puncture, caused by bashing the wheel into something so hard that it pinches the inner tube and splits it

taco wheel that has been badly bent in a crash

wild pigs badly adjusted brakes that squeal when used

wipeout crash

Finding Out More

THE INTERNET

www.uci.ch
The home site of the Union Cycliste Internationale, the governing body of cycle sports. Click on "BMX" or "Mountain biking" to get information about top-level competitions, world rankings, the basics of each sport, and more.

www.nyskatespots.com
If you're going to New York, this online guide helps you locate skate and BMX spots in specific areas.

BOOKS

Diary of a BMX Freak Paul Mason (Heinemann Library, 2004)
Extracts from the diary of a young man who goes from being a complete BMX beginner to coming third in a big local competition.

To the Limit: Mountain Biking Paul Mason (Wayland, 2008)
An excellent introduction to mountain biking, including basic kit, bikes, techniques, and some famous riders.

BMX Riding Skills: The Guide to Flatland Tricks Shek Hon (Firefly Books, 2010)
Does what it says on the cover: an exhaustive guide to a huge variety of flatland tricks, from beginner to expert level. Written by one of the best flatland riders in the UK.

MAGAZINES

Ride UK BMX
One of the UK's biggest and best BMX magazines, *Ride UK* carries articles on BMX spots, techniques, personalities, equipment and competition. It also has a good website, at **http://rideukbmx.com**.

Dig BMX
Similar content to *Ride UK BMX*, but with its own slant on people and events. Also has a website, at **http://digbmx.com**.

Index

aerials 18, 19
Afan Valley, Wales 16–17
Antelope Wells, USA 24
Australian National
    Championships 20

Banff, Canada 24
Barcelona, Spain 27
Beijing Olympics, 2008 23
berms 4, 5, 10, 23
Bike City 22
bivouac 24, 25
Blue Mountains, Australia 7
BMX 4, 5, 8, 9, 14, 15, 18, 19,
    22, 23, 26, 27
    dirt jump 9, 18, 19
    flatland 18, 19, 26, 27
    mini ramp 18, 19
    park 9, 18, 19, 26
    racing 8, 9, 15, 22, 23
    street 8, 9, 15, 26
    vert ramp 18, 19
BMX bikes 5
BMX etiquette 27
BMX supercross 22, 23
BMX Worlds 18–19
Brooklyn Banks, New York,
    USA 26, 27

cadence 13, 17
Camp Woodward, USA 9,
    14–15, 19
Chula Vista, USA 23
Copenhagen, Denmark 22–23
cornering 21

Decoy, England 8–9
Durango, USA 12–13

fire roads 16, 17
Forte, Kye 9
Fréjus, France 23

Glentress, Scotland 16
grinds 19, 27

helmet 8, 11, 21
hole shot 23

Innerleithen, Scotland 20

Josa, Danny 18
Jugendpark, Germany 19

Kranskja Gora, Slovenia 20

Laggan Wolftrax, Scotland 7
Les Deux Alpes, France 28–29
London, England 27

Madrid, Spain 23
Marin County, USA 6–7
Mount Beauty, Australia 20–21
mountain bikes 5, 6, 7, 11, 29
mountain biking 5, 6, 10, 11,
    12, 13, 16, 17, 20, 21, 24,
    25, 28, 29
    cross country (XC) 6, 11, 12,
    13, 16, 20, 21, 28, 29
    downhill 5, 11, 12, 20, 28, 29
    freeriding 10, 11, 28

Napolitan, Anthony 19
New York City, USA 26–27

ollie 4, 5, 9

pegs 8, 9, 27
police 26, 27
pro riders 15

quick releases 29

rails 26
riding downhill 11, 12, 13, 21,
    28, 29
riding uphill 13, 17

Semmering, Austria 10–11
Sierra Nevada, Spain 13
singletracks 7, 13, 16, 17, 20
sizing a bike 7
Squamish, Canada 16
start ramp 22, 23

Tompkins Square Park, New
    York, USA 27
Tour Divide MTB Race 24–25
TransRockies race, Canada 25
TransScotland race 25
TransWales race 25

Vancouver Island, Canada 11

Whistler, Canada 29
Woodward West, USA 9, 15

Aberdeenshire
COUNCIL

Aberdeenshire Library and Information Service
www.aberdeenshire.gov.uk/libraries
Renewals Hotline 01224 661511

A L I S

3026368